DO YOU WANT A CAREER IN CRIMINAL JUSTICE?

JOBS IN THE
CORRECTIONS
SYSTEM

KATHLEEN A. KLATTE

ROSEN
PUBLISHING

NEW YORK

Published in 2022 by The Rosen Publishing Group, Inc.
29 East 21st Street, New York, NY 10010

Copyright © 2022 by The Rosen Publishing Group, Inc.

First Edition

Portions of this work were originally authored by Daniel E. Harmon and published as *Careers in the Corrections System*. All new material in this edition was authored by Kathleen A. Klatte.

Cataloging-in-Publication Data

Names: Klatte, Kathleen A.
Title: Jobs in the corrections system / Kathleen A. Klatte.
Description: New York : Rosen Publishing, 2022. | Series: Do you want a career in criminal justice? | Includes glossary and index.
Identifiers: ISBN 9781499470079 (pbk.) | ISBN 9781499470086 (library bound) | ISBN 9781499470093 (ebook)
Subjects: LCSH: Corrections--Vocational guidance--United States--Juvenile literature.
Classification: LCC HV9471.K48 2022 | DDC 364.6023'73--dc23

Some of the images in this book illustrate individuals who are models. The depictions do not imply actual situations or events.

Manufactured in the United States of America

CPSIA Compliance Information: Batch #CSRYA22. For further information contact Rosen Publishing, New York, New York at 1-800-237-9932.

Find us on

CONTENTS

INTRODUCTION

M ost people who pursue careers in law enforcement are interested in preventing crimes, solving mysteries, catching criminals, or bringing wrongdoers to justice. In the corrections system, the crimes already have been solved and the criminals already have been caught, tried, and sentenced. The main task of a corrections professional is to help administer the punishment process securely, humanely, effectively, and with a view toward someday returning incarcerated individuals to a productive life in society when possible. It's a rewarding career path—but one with unavoidable risks.

Qualified corrections professionals are always in demand for the simple, sad reason that people continue to violate laws and require correctional supervision. Although statistics show that the number of people under correctional supervision is dropping, many prisons are overcrowded or out of date. Newspaper reports and television documentaries frequently describe dangerous overcrowding in jails and prisons throughout the United States. New facilities equipped with the latest technology are constantly being built to replace outdated buildings and house inmate populations. Additional trained staff members are needed to operate them.

Surveys made by the Bureau of Justice Statistics, part of the U.S. Department of Justice, show that 6.4 million adults had been under correctional supervision in the United States at some point in

Although prison guard is probably the first job that comes to mind, there's a need for many other types of professionals in the corrections system.

2018. That meant one in forty adults was an offender within the corrections system. The 2018 total was a decrease of about 140,000 offenders from the 2017 statistics.

Of the number of supervised offenders at the end of 2018, about 4.4 million were living in the community, on probation or parole. The others were housed in prisons, local jails, or other detention facilities, or were being supervised at halfway houses and in alternative punishment programs.

Not all corrections officers are prison guards. Counseling and supervisory employees work constantly with both inmates and those who have been released on probation or parole. Needed professionals include specialists who have management, clerical, psychological, medical, and other forms of training. Every job category calls for dedicated employees who possess a combination of the right skills, education, talents, interests, and attitude to make an effective corrections officer.

If a corrections worker performs with dedication, job security is practically assured. However, many workers eventually decide to abandon their careers. Turnover is common because the job—especially for corrections officers who are in daily contact with dangerous criminals—can be highly stressful.

Although the number of convicted offenders is disturbing and staff burnout often occurs, aspiring corrections workers can be excited about the opportunities for them to make a positive impact. Regardless of their job titles, if they perform well, corrections workers contribute to a better society. In recent years, the push for rehabilitation over incarceration has resulted in many positive changes in the U.S. corrections system. The system strives to rehabilitate criminals so that they may rejoin society in a productive and just capacity. Corrections officers and other workers in the corrections system are needed to help make this transition successful. Because of what they do, lives that have gone astray can be changed dramatically for the better.

CHAPTER 1

A LARGE AND COMPLEX SYSTEM

The corrections system is a dynamic web of organizations. It exists to carry out the sentences assigned to convicted criminals. It functions to protect society from violent offenders and attempts to rehabilitate people convicted of nonviolent or minor offenses.

The sentences imposed by the court system and carried out by the corrections system range from fines or community service for minor offenses to incarceration or even execution for serious violent crimes. Psychiatric care, education, pastoral care, and recovery from substance abuse are all part of the modern corrections system. These services require a wide variety of professionals.

Unfortunately, there will always be violent offenders who need to be separated from society, and individuals trained in security will be required to guard them.

While the population under correctional supervision is increasing in some states, it's decreasing in others. Some states are changing laws so there are options besides incarceration for less serious offenses. It can be less expensive and more productive overall to rehabilitate an offender so they can be a functioning member of society. This population includes individuals incarcerated in prison facilities with varying levels of security, as well as individuals supervised in the community.

The corrections system offers a wide variety of career opportunities for people interested in making a difference in their community. Though challenging, these careers can also be very rewarding.

A PUNISHMENT TO FIT THE CRIME

When people are convicted of wrongdoing, they don't all go through the same correctional processes. The sentencing judge may commit them to one of many different programs or facilities. For the simplest misdemeanors—speeding violations or possession of marijuana, for example—there may be hardly any correctional process at all beyond, perhaps, a lecture from the judge. The guilty person might be ordered to pay a light fine or may be dismissed with simply a warning. A vandal might be ordered to pay restitution for property that was damaged or lost. An accessory to a crime might be penalized by forfeiture—being forced to give up certain property that was used in an illegal act (an automobile or weapon, for instance).

State laws specify the appropriate range of punishment for different crimes. Laws vary from state to state. For example, there are two kinds of larceny (theft), which are defined by the value of the stolen property. Grand larceny, involving higher values, is a felony that can result in imprisonment. Petit (petty, or minor) theft is a misdemeanor that might be dismissed with a fine and/or probation. The dividing line, in terms of stolen property value, is not the same in every state. The same amount of stolen goods can land a culprit in prison in one state but bring only a rap on the knuckles in another. Meanwhile, the highest form of punishment—the death penalty—is allowed in 27 states, as of 2021, but is shunned in the others, where life imprisonment without parole is the maximum sentence. The U.S. federal government and the U.S. military also permit the death penalty.

If more than an immediate fine or payment of restitution is called for, the guilty party enters the corrections system. Not all forms of correction require confinement, but they all impose account- ability. At the least, they require the wrongdoer to demonstrate an understanding of the error and an intention to go straight.

Non-confinement components of the corrections system are twofold: probation and parole. Probation means the person can go free immediately after conviction—under certain conditions. The judge typically announces a jail or prison sentence (or a hefty fine), but in the same order reduces the sentence to probation (a brief period of incarceration, followed by a longer term of probation). The guilty person who is willing to meet the terms of probation can avoid the formidable fine or confinement. But if during the probationary period the person violates any of the conditions of the court order, the court may reinstate the original, heavier sentence.

What are the terms of probation? The person must regularly meet with a probation officer and answer questions about any personal activities from day to day, including events at work or during recreational times. If the subject is found to be lying or commits another crime while on probation, freedom may be taken away. Depending on the crime, other conditions may be imposed. If the person completes the probationary period without incident, the correctional process is completed.

Judges are most likely to reduce a sentence to probation for first-time offenders and youthful offenders. The reasoning is that if a violator's wrongdoing results from an impulsive, thoughtless act or from immaturity, the community is better served in the long run by giving the person another chance. Incarceration not only can cast the first-time offender among hardened felons, it will also cost

Offenders on probation must meet with their probation officer regularly, as well as follow guidelines set by the court.

the state a significant amount of money to keep the individual confined.

Probation is granted immediately after a person's conviction, during the sentencing phase. Parole, by contrast, applies at the further end of the correctional process. It's a shortening of the sentence, often due to good behavior while in prison, after a prisoner has served a portion of it.

In many criminal cases, a sentencing judge issues an indeterminate sentence—not a specified number of months or years, but a time frame—during which justice can be satisfied. An indeterminate sentence might specify "two to six years" of incarceration. The decision of exactly how long the inmate will serve is left to the parole board of that jurisdiction. The board periodically reviews the prisoner's records and interviews the prisoner, as well as individuals who may have an impact on an early release decision. In many cases, if the inmate has a record of good behavior while serving time, the board will grant a parole. The prisoner is released before the maximum sentence is carried out but remains accountable to a parole officer. The released inmate must report regularly, much like the person on probation. Depending on conditions of the parole, the inmate might, for example, be forbidden to leave the state during the parole period. If the parolee is convicted of another crime during the parole period, the original sentence will be reinstated, in addition to sentencing for the new offense.

When an offender is considered for parole, a hearing is held to determine if they're safe to be returned to the community.

Both probation and parole processes require specially trained professionals within the corrections system. They must manage their cases carefully and determine whether the individual is truly fit to be free in the community. In some cases, they recommend that probation or parole be reversed.

O.J. SIMPSON'S PAROLE HEARING

In 2017, former football star O.J. Simpson was eligible for parole after serving nine years of a nine- to thirty-three-year sentence for armed robbery and other charges. In some ways, it was a textbook parole hearing. Simpson had served the minimum amount of prison time. He was older and technically a first-time offender. He was incarcerated in a medium-security facility with no disciplinary issues.

One challenge of Simpson's legal proceedings was to confine matters to the crime in question. Of course, this was difficult due to the notoriety surrounding the deaths of Nicole Brown Simpson and Ron Goldman.

Simpson is expected to serve five years of parole. Despite his fame, Simpson's parole will be similar to any other offenders. He must meet with his parole officer on a regular basis. He's subject to being searched or ordered to take a drug test. Due to his age, he's not required to hold a job. He may not leave the state without permission. Violation of the terms of his parole can be cause for him to return to prison.

Corrections professionals played many roles in Simpson's plea for parole. Guards and mental health professionals inside the facility had to compile reports of his behavior and activities while confined. Lawyers had to determine if he fit the legal criteria for parole. Once he's back in the community, he will be supervised by a parole officer to be sure he's abiding by the terms of his release and making good choices to ensure his future as a member of society.

INCARCERATION

The main objective of a facility of incarceration is to keep convicted criminals away from society at large. But while doing that, the prison or detention center must provide proper housing and care for inmates. It must see that their basic human rights aren't violated.

Jails are short-term places of confinement. They're not designed to house an inmate for longer than a few days, weeks, or months. The inmate capacity of most jails is no more than 100, although some jails are larger and, at times, are forced to house 1,000 or more prisoners.

Many jail inmates are people who've been arrested and charged with a crime and are awaiting their day in court. Others have been tried and convicted—or they pleaded guilty—and sentenced to short periods of confinement. Convicted felons who've been sentenced to longer prison terms are sometimes held temporarily in jails until correctional authorities can find them a permanent place at larger prisons.

Prisons, operated by state or federal governments, are intended to house felons who must serve longer sentences. Not all prisons are alike. Different facilities are designed to accommodate different types of criminals. Maximum-security prisons house those who are considered the most dangerous. Inside them, some inmates, because of dangerously violent personalities or the nature of the crimes they committed, are kept apart from the general prison population.

SMALL-TOWN JAILS

Jails are meant to provide short-term incarceration, generally while offenders are awaiting their day in court or serving a short sentence. They're not designed or intended for long-term detention. While the overall prison population is dropping, populations of rural jails are increasing.

In some cases, this is because the accused can't afford bail. In others, it's because there are a small number of judges responsible for a large geographical area. Prisoners awaiting a hearing can wait for months for a judge to arrive to hear their case.

Some rural communities see the construction of a new jail as having positive economic impact. Jails provide jobs for the community, as well as a market for supplies. Rural jails can also contract with other agencies in need of housing for incarcerated populations. For example, border patrol agencies sometimes require additional housing for immigrants awaiting deportation.

San Quentin State Prison is the oldest prison in California. It's the facility where executions were carried out until 2019. That year, governor Gavin Newsom placed a moratorium on the death penalty in California.

One institution especially noted for its infamous residents is California State Prison, Corcoran. Inmates in its Protective Housing Unit included Charles Manson, who directed his cult "family" to carry out multiple, gruesome murders in 1969. Another resident of the unit was Juan Corona, convicted of murdering 25 itinerant farm workers in 1971.

Due to the horrific nature of the murders Manson directed, he was initially sentenced to death. The sentence was commuted to life imprisonment. He died in prison in 2017.

At the highest security level—"super-maximum" prisons or "control units"—extremely dangerous criminals are kept in solitary confinement most of the day. When they're released from their cells, they're shackled.

Minimum-security institutions house those who've committed less serious crimes and who aren't considered dangerous to society. In some minimum-security environments, prisoners enjoy certain freedoms and comforts inside the prison and may even be allowed weekend visits outside.

Between maximum and minimum security are different levels of severity. Special detention facilities house juvenile inmates and certain types of law-breakers who require special treatment, such as disabled or substance-dependent individuals. Near the end of their sentences, many prisoners are allowed to complete their terms in halfway houses. These are supervised homes within the community where inmates can gradually adjust and reenter society.

In some cases, convicted individuals may not have to serve inside institutions alongside more serious offenders, but they may lose some of their freedoms. They might be confined to their homes under the custody of relatives, for example, or they might have to wear electronic monitoring devices. Their sentence may consist of reporting for community service work each weekend for a period of time.

Home confinement isn't just for petty or first-time offenders—it's also used as a step toward a longtime prisoner's reentry into the community. The Federal

Ankle monitors are one of the tools available to corrections officers. They can be used to monitor offenders who are residing in the community under supervision.

Bureau of Prisons frequently places inmates on home confinement as they approach the end of their terms (within the final six months or 10 percent of their sentence periods). During this prerelease time, most prisoners are expected to find jobs and are required to remain at home when they're not working. The objective of the program, the bureau explains, is to provide "an opportunity for inmates to assume increasing levels of responsibility, while, at the same time, providing sufficient restrictions to promote community safety and convey the sanctioning value of the sentence."

PUBLIC VS. PRIVATE

The corrections system is an ever-evolving field with plenty of opportunities for civic-minded individuals. Most prisons are government run, and most corrections professionals are civil servants, with government salaries and benefits. They are also subject to government oversight.

Some states, such as New York, are overhauling their criminal justice systems. The objective is to prevent the mass incarceration of first-time offenders and persons convicted of relatively minor crimes. They'll still require professional supervision and rehabilitation in the community. This facilitates the goal of rehabilitating offenders and reintegrating them into society, rather than "warehousing" them. There is also the concern that exposing comparatively nonviolent offenders to the often-violent environment of prison is detrimental.

There will always be a need for security personnel to guard dangerous offenders who must be separated from society. However, even the most desperate criminals are still entitled to fundamental human rights. Offenders are entitled to food and medical care. Psychiatric care and substance abuse rehabilitation are in the best interests of the prisoners, staff, and society at large. Maximum security facilities require trained counselors, mental health professionals, clergy, nutritionists, and doctors.

The American Civil Liberties Union (ACLU) has focused attention on the poor conditions in American prisons, and the rights of incarcerated offenders. Individuals considering a career in corrections should think about the rehabilitation aspects of the field, as there is considerable public attention on this facet of the system.

There's also the matter of privately owned "for-profit" prisons. The first private prisons appeared in the early 1980s, in connection with the "war on drugs." It was thought at the time that privately owned and operated facilities would be more cost effective than government institutions.

As of 2019, private prisons housed 7 percent of state prisoners and 16 percent of federal prisoners in the United States. Private prisons are located primarily in the southern and western states. There are concerns that these facilities are unconstitutional, as punishing law breakers is the purview of the government. Some states, such as New York, have gone so far as to ban private prisons. Still, private security facilities do provide some additional employment for corrections professionals.

WHERE DO I FIND THE JOBS?

Employment in the corrections system and opportunities for advancement vary by location. Calls for prison reform and an overhaul of the system tend to be more prevalent in urban areas. In New York, extensive reforms are underway, resulting in the closure of facilities. The focus of the system is on rehabilitation and reintegration, rather than incarceration. The state has also expanded services for juvenile offenders to break the cycle of criminal behavior.

California offers an interesting alternative for minimum-security offenders who meet certain criteria. They may volunteer to participate in Conservation Camps, where they become certified to fight brush fires. Corrections officers who oversee the camps receive special training, as the inmates must be supervised even while fighting fires or mitigating floods. The camps also offer education and rehabilitation programs.

CHAPTER 2

INSIDE PRISON WALLS

Prison guard is the occupation most people associate with the idea of a career in corrections. These are the professionals with the most direct contact with inmates. Specific duties will vary depending on the size, location, and nature of the facility. Generally, corrections officers are responsible for guarding prisoners and overseeing their activities. This might include dangerous activities such as breaking up fights or searching for contraband. It can also include more mundane assignments such as completing paperwork and reports. Corrections officers must always be alert and prepared to respond to violent or emergency situations.

According to the Occupational Outlook Handbook, approximately half a million people were employed as corrections workers or bailiffs in 2019. The median pay for corrections workers is about $45,000 per year.

Corrections officers work in a high-stress environment. Correctional facilities operate 24 hours a day, 365 days of the year. They must be fully staffed on holidays, during extreme weather, and any other extraordinary circumstance. There's a high rate of job-related injury and illness, as well as considerable burnout due to stress. It can be a rewarding career, but one that should be carefully considered.

NOT A FUN PLACE

No jail or prison is a relaxing place to live or work. Many prisoners are noisy and aggressive. TVs and radios blare throughout the cell blocks. Most facilities are overcrowded. As of October 2020, institutions in the California Department of Corrections and Rehabilitation were operating at 108 percent of their design capacity. Many prisons are outdated—poorly ventilated and badly lit, with frequent plumbing and structural problems. Tempers flare easily among inmates.

Because of this, corrections officers are always on guard. They must be especially alert when inmates are together in common areas—dining halls, showers, and exercise grounds. Even when the surroundings seem calm, corrections profes-

The California Institution for Men at Chino was one of the first minimum-security prisons built in the United States.

sionals know the inmates are living under duress. This tension extends to the prison work staff. Guards must always be mindful of what's going on among prisoners, watching for signs of danger. They come to know prisoners' individual traits. They're aware of the subcultures that exist within the inmate population—the gangs, the group leaders, the potential troublemakers, and the coded signals gang members use to communicate.

Most prisoners who enter the corrections system just want to serve their sentences and return to free society as soon as possible. They're not troublemakers by nature. But other inmates have violent or domineering personality traits. This results in a very complex social structure within the prison population. It produces power struggles and clashes among racial and special-interest factions. Corrections officers are required to maintain control. Sometimes, they have to use force to keep order.

A racial conflict apparently sparked a series of riots in the Los Angeles County, California, jail system in 2006. At least one inmate died and many more suffered injuries ranging from slight to serious. Prisoners elsewhere have reacted violently to matters as seemingly trivial as clothing. An incident of this kind occurred at a privately operated prison in New Castle, Indiana, in 2007. Inmates from Arizona, unhappy with their relocation to the Indiana prison, refused to wear issued clothing at lunchtime. When members of the corrections staff confronted them, they responded violently. A corrections supervisor was beaten, and seven inmates and two guards received minor injuries.

PRISON RIOTS

Perhaps the most infamous prison riot in American history occurred at the Attica Correctional Facility in New York in 1971. Although some of the inmates' complaints were reasonable—concerning overcrowded and unsanitary living conditions—these issues were allowed to fester until violence erupted the morning of September 9. After four days of failed negotiations, authorities ended the uprising by force, resulting in many casualties.

In 2018, gang activity sparked a riot at a South Carolina facility. Corrections officers must always be alert for the possibility of violence. In this case, inmates continued their gang-related activities while incarcerated, using smuggled cell phones to communicate with gang members outside the prison.

It may seem surprising that in many correctional settings, officers are unarmed when they're in direct contact with prisoners. One reason for this is for officers to avoid the risk of losing their weapons in the event of a group attack. However, inmate movements are under perpetual surveillance, and outside colleagues are ready to assist quickly should trouble occur.

A select few corrections professionals are specially trained for tactical response teams, also called special reaction teams. These units deal with riots, hostage crises, the forced removal of inmates from cells or other areas, and other dangerous situations. Besides advanced training in weapons (including the use of tear gas, rubber bullets, and grenades) and

A specially trained tactical team in full gear is practicing a drill for subduing a riot. Corrections officers must always be alert and prepared to handle any contingency.

self-defense, they must have knowledge of potential threats such as poisons and other chemical agents.

NOT JUST GUARDS

A corrections officer at any institution—federal or state prison, city or county jail, or special facility for youthful offenders or those with psychiatric or substance abuse problems—must perform multiple tasks. It's by no means a matter of simply carrying a gun and monitoring inmates' behavior.

The duties of corrections officers might include the following:

- Conducting frequent head counts among prisoners
- Ensuring exterior gate and interior door security
- Inspecting the facility—especially entrances, windows, and locks
- Serving as guards and tower sentries (sentries, armed with rifles, are selected for their superior marksmanship)
- Receiving and processing incoming prisoners, including fingerprinting or photographing the offenders for record files
- Labeling and storing new arrivals' belongings that are not allowed inside a cell

Some corrections officers are trained investigators who can probe crimes that are committed inside the prison. Transportation officers bring new inmates into the compound and are trained to securely transport prisoners who are scheduled for court appearances or parole hearings, or who require hospitalization outside the prison. Other

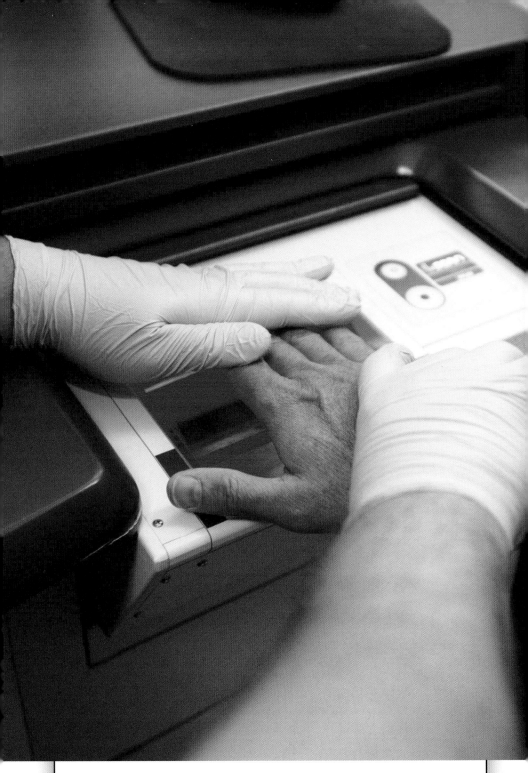

This corrections officer is scanning the palm of an incoming prisoner. This technology reads the unique pattern of veins in a subject's hand.

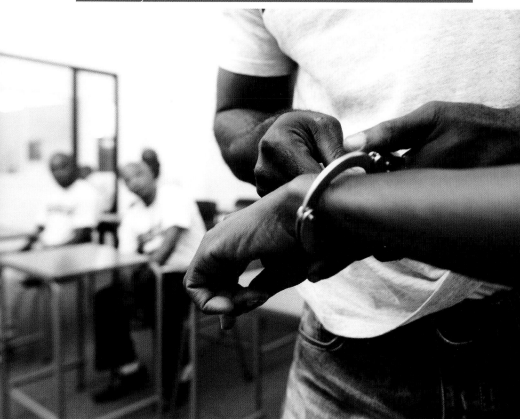

Prospective corrections professionals usually attend a training academy, then serve several months of on-the-job training before they're considered full-fledged officers.

officers constantly monitor inmates via surveillance cameras. Prisoners are under watchful eyes while they're eating, exercising, lounging, bathing, working—and even sleeping.

There are also routine duties: keeping daily records of prisoner activities, monitoring and distributing mail to inmates, providing them with toiletries and other necessities, monitoring visitation, and accompanying inmates to educational classes and work assignments inside the institution.

At some county and municipal jails, jailers are not career corrections officers but are new deputies or police officers who are assigned to guard duty. This specified task gives them experience with the criminal element within a controlled setting before they're sent out on patrol. During this period, some law enforcement rookies decide they want to devote their careers to corrections, rather than to public police duty.

WHICH JURISDICTION?

Corrections officers are needed at every kind of facility, and those needs are growing. Although job tasks may be similar at each level of government facility—federal, state, and local—the required education and experience are not the same. Nor are the pay scales or the prospects for promotion.

At the federal level, corrections officers are needed not just inside federal prisons but at other agencies. The Department of Homeland Security (DHS) employs a trained corrections staff as part of one of its agencies, U.S. Immigration and Customs Enforcement (ICE). This includes armed officials who must temporarily detain people suspected of citizenship violations. The DHS and ICE were created following the events of 9/11 to prevent terrorists from entering the country through immigration channels.

The Bureau of Indian Affairs also needs corrections workers. These officers work on tribal lands, and preference is given to qualified Native American candidates. The Department of the Interior (DOI) employs Park Police and investigators who must sometimes detain, process, and counsel individuals who are arrested at park sites. They sometimes work in remote locations, protecting natural resources in the National Park Service. Most DOI corrections personnel—like those in other agencies that are not primarily concerned with detention and correction— are law enforcement officers who can also perform correctional duties, as needed.

Corrections specialists also work in the military branches, which are part of the federal government. And the U.S. Marshals Service (under the Department of Justice) needs corrections professionals to house, transport, and oversee prisoners who've been arrested by the FBI and other federal law enforcement agencies. U.S. marshals are responsible for the accused individuals' security until their day in court.

The daily tasks of corrections officers in federal institutions are much the same as those of workers in state prisons. However, prisoners convicted of federal crimes are, for the most part, considered especially threatening to society.

Federal corrections jobs pay more than those at state and local facilities. Not surprisingly, they have greater requirements. Whereas many state and municipal institutions require only a high school diploma for applicants to entry-level positions, federal jobs are more likely to call for either a four-year college degree, or a combination of college credits and experience. Most federal jobs also require spe-

U.S. Marshals often handle prisoners such as terrorists who are considered high profile or extremely dangerous. They must be alert for possible escapes or attempts at vigilante justice.

cial security clearance, which entails more stringent testing and background checks of applicants than those for state or local positions.

A HIGH-STRESS ENVIRONMENT

The best corrections officers treat prisoners with respect and even with a degree of friendliness. They win respect from some of the inmates in return. They provide job information and advice that can help offenders readjust to society after their releases. These are some of the personal services they can provide, and the later testimonies of offenders who benefited from their help are the foremost rewards of their jobs.

However, officers know they can never become too friendly with prisoners. They know where to draw the line between friend and guard. They understand how the criminal mind works and how some people in confinement are masters of manipulation. And they know that many of the prisoners they oversee, although they might appear friendly on the surface, resent them simply because corrections officers represent authority.

Aspiring corrections officers should consider other worrisome aspects of the job before proceeding into this career path. Corrections officers typically work eight-hour shifts—and the shifts change. The officer will work regular daytime hours for a while, then rotate to evening hours, then to early-morning hours. Expect to share weekend and holiday

PUPPIES FOR PAROLE

Puppies for Parole (P4P) is a rehabilitation program used by the Missouri Department of Corrections. Certain offenders at 19 institutions throughout the state are eligible for the program. The inmates receive training and the opportunity to be certified as animal handlers, which can help them to become employed after their release.

The program aids the community by providing trained dogs for adoption through local shelters. It reduces the number of dogs euthanized or languishing in shelters. More than 6,000 dogs had been adopted through the program since it started in 2010. The Advanced Puppies for Parole program trains helper dogs and therapy dogs, some of which are used to help children testifying in the court system.

The P4P program aids the correctional institution by teaching skills that help the offender to return to society. The presence of the dogs also aids the morale and mental state of inmates and staff alike. It's also an incentive for continued good behavior on the part of the inmates, making the facility safer for everyone.

obligations with colleagues. Correctional facilities never close, and supervision must be constant. Every employee takes part in the 24/7/365 regimen. Many correctional facilities are in rural, isolated locations. That means many employees face the annoyance and expense of long commutes to and from work.

INSIDE THE COURTHOUSE

Some corrections-related security tasks are performed outside prisons and jails. In courthouses (all levels of criminal court), bailiffs are the officers responsible for keeping order and ensuring the protection of everyone in the courtroom. They escort juries between the courtroom and the deliberation chamber, to lunch, and—in lengthy trials—to and from court-arranged lodgings. They search people entering the courtroom for weapons and keep a watchful eye for suspicious behavior during proceedings. They silence or oust talkers and cell phone users. Two or more bailiffs usually serve together.

Bailiffs are officers of the court. In most situations, however, they're paid by a related law enforcement agency. The U.S. Marshals Service oversees federal court bailiffs. State or circuit court bailiffs are provided by the sheriff's department of the county in which the courthouse is located. Municipal court bailiffs are paid by the city or town police department. A detachment of armed law enforcement officers almost always is present to assist bailiffs when criminal court is in session. The median pay for bailiffs in 2019 was about $47,000. Since courts are not constantly in session, many bailiffs are hired part-time. Others are full-time law enforcement personnel assigned temporarily to serve a court as corrections officers.

Besides maintaining order when court is in session, the bailiff is responsible for overseeing courtroom maintenance. This includes every detail, including electrical systems, lighting, and sanitation. Bailiffs also run errands for judges, other court officials, and jury members.

CORRECTIONS CAREERS FOR WOMEN

Until the mid-1900s, almost all corrections officers were men. They were taught not to let prisoners or parolees "get out of line." To make sure they kept control, they didn't hesitate to use physical force, sometimes brutally. This sort of behavior is considered unacceptable today.

Women have been part of prison systems for centuries, but their roles have been limited. In times past, they were hired only to perform clerical work (typing or record keeping), nursing, and classroom instruction. Some were responsible for keeping the guards' arsenal of weapons in top condition. The few who were armed and trained as guards were assigned to surveillance towers, away from immediate prisoner contact in the grounds and cell blocks.

Men and women of different races make up today's security staffs inside prisons and detention centers. A court ruling in 1982 forbade discrimination against women applicants for all corrections roles. At about the same time, the percentage of female prisoners in the United States began to climb significantly. More than 107,000 women were in confinement at the end of 2019, according to the Bureau of Justice Statistics. Women corrections offi-

In less than a century, women have progressed from not being allowed to work as corrections officers to reaching the highest echelon of the profession: prison warden.

cers at all levels have found a growing demand for their services. Some have risen to the top corrections career position of prison warden.

HOW FAR CAN YOU GO?

A career as a corrections officer has plenty of room for advancement. Corrections sergeant is a supervisory position. With dedication, integrity, and a willingness to continue one's education, an administrative position such as warden is a worthy career goal.

Some people who start out as corrections officers later decide that they're better suited for a different aspect of criminal justice, perhaps supervising offenders in the community or even in a courthouse. Again, a willingness to seek out further education and professional certifications is essential. Experience as a corrections officer can be the basis for a distinguished career.

CHAPTER 3

SO MANY PATHS TO CHOOSE FROM

I t takes much more than guards with guns to maintain a secure corrections facility in the 21st century. Buildings must be specially designed to provide suitable security for violent offenders while still providing for humane considerations such as adequate heating, cooling, and ventilation. Cooks and nutritionists must provide meals that account for the medical issues and religious restrictions of a large and mixed population. Doctors, dentists, and substance abuse counselors are required to deal with medical issues that inmates arrive with, as well as injuries from fights and accidents.

Modern facilities need IT specialists and office administrators. Chaplains and counselors attend to inmates' spiritual and emotional needs. Educators and social workers try to prepare offenders to rejoin society. Almost any career path you can think of can be applied to the corrections system.

HOW MANY MORE JOBS CAN YOU THINK OF?

- Architect
- Caseworker
- Chaplain
- Clerical Worker
- Cook
- Dentist
- Doctor
- Facility Manager
- Guard
- Janitor
- IT Specialist
- Lawyer
- Nutritionist
- Public Relations Specialist
- Social Worker
- Teacher
- Therapist
- Warden

COMMUNITY SUPERVISION

Most convicted criminals in the United States are not incarcerated. They're either out on probation or out on parole. That means the courts and corrections authorities deem them to be safe members of ordinary society—but they must follow specified rules of conduct and report regularly to their probation or parole officers. More than 91,000 probation officers and correctional treatment specialists were employed in federal, state, and local corrections systems in 2019, according to the Bureau of Labor Statistics. The number of available jobs in probation may increase by as much as 4 percent by 2029, according to the bureau. The job market for parole officers is more limited.

Probation and parole officers need skills that aren't required of other corrections professionals. They must be a combination of supervisor, counselor, investigator, effective communicator, careful observer, and paper shuffler. They must have computer skills and be able to write thorough, clear reports on their clients' progress during the supervisory period. A bachelor's degree and the ability to speak Spanish are helpful. Probation officers are a bit like police officers, but more like social workers.

Probation officers are assigned by the court to supervise offenders with suspended sentences. But beforehand, they may be called on to investigate the case and the offender's background prior to sentencing and to advise the court as to an appropriate sentence. They check the criminal and employment histories of the convicted person, talk to victims, and talk to arresting officers. They interview relatives, medical or counseling professionals, and others who may have insight about the individual. The information they glean can affect the nature and severity of the sentence. In some instances, the probation officer concludes that the offender is unlikely to comply with probation orders and advises the court to that effect.

NOT AS SEEN ON TV

Television and movies tend to portray prisons as dank, bleak places where terrible things happen. While this might have been true once, modern criminal justice reforms seek to make prisons cleaner and healthier. Of course, keeping the facility secure will always be the main concern, but studies have shown that increasing the amount of natural light and introducing colors is better for the mental health of everyone in the facility—staff and inmates alike. This, in turn, makes the facility safer.

Modern prisons are designed by specialty architectural firms. They consult with experts in security, mental health, and human behavior to design safe, secure, and sanitary buildings. Air quality is also a concern, as prisons have historically been breeding grounds for contagious disease.

Probation officers are checking on a convicted sex offender on Halloween. They're making sure he's at home and not in contact with children.

If probation is the sentence, the court often requires that the offender pay a fine or make restitution to victims or perform community service work (usually on weekends). A rehabilitation plan might require various forms of counseling. It might forbid the offender from associating with specified friends or associates who, in the opinion of the court, could lead the offender astray—or who, on the other hand, might be victimized by the offender. The probation officer is responsible for seeing that the terms of release are met. If they aren't, the officer might recommend that probation be revoked and that the full sentence be imposed. Probation officers are sometimes called to deal with violations and other problems late at night and on weekends.

Since most of those on probation are young people or first-time offenders, many probation jobs deal with juveniles. Some youthful offenders are especially rebellious, arrogant, manipulative, and uncooperative.

Parole officers likewise work with offenders who've been released into society, but their cases are quite different from those usually assigned to probation workers. A large part of their contribution to society is to help veteran inmates adjust as they reenter the community. The parole period usually extends until the end of the prisoner's original sentence. For example, an offender may be sentenced to between two and six years in prison. At the end of three years, the parole board may grant a release. The prisoner is free but is under parole—held accountable to the parole officer and to the terms of prerelease—for the remaining three years of the sentence. Hopefully, by that time, the offender will have become a law-abiding citizen who is contributing to society and won't return to crime.

To see that this happens, the parole officer tries to help the released offender find a meaningful job and, if necessary, a stable home. The parolee may need substance abuse counseling, job training, or psychiatric help. Periodically (several times per week or month, depending on the parole terms and on the officer's caseload), the officer and offender meet to discuss concerns. From time to time, the parole officer will confer with the client's relatives, acquaintances, and employer to stay apprised of the individual's progress.

Careful case notes are important here, as they are with probation clients. The parolee's performance during the release period must be reported periodically to the parole board.

Like probation officers, parole officers are sometimes assigned in advance to investigate a promising inmate's records and personal situation, such as home life and job prospects, and to advise the parole board whether an early release is wise. This investigation may include interviews with corrections officers and other prison employees to discuss the inmate's behavior.

Offenders who are out on probation have a strong incentive to comply with the terms, because if they don't, the court may order them to serve their full prison sentences. Offenders who violate parole know that if they're caught, they will be returned to confinement—likely with additional penalties for parole violations.

Too often, though, offenders who are free on probation or parole don't follow the rules. Some fail to report regularly and refuse to be held accountable. Some relocate to other cities or states and ignore their release terms altogether. And many resume criminal activities.

Some probation and parole officers are armed and authorized to apprehend violators. In most cases, though, they can't physically force their clients to obey court orders because the offenders are not confined and can leave the area. But if and when the violators are rearrested, the reports of their supervising corrections officials will have a considerable bearing on their future sentencing.

Perhaps the most difficult part of the probation or parole officer's job is the caseload. Most government agencies are stingy about hiring additional workers in the area of corrections; they do so only when necessary. Probation and parole officers thus find themselves overwhelmed with clients. This heavy caseload makes for long hours and impaired work quality because they can't afford to spend too much time on any single case.

GETTING LIVES BACK ON TRACK

Inside the jail and prison setting, numerous professionals are at work for the benefit of the inmates. They include psychologists who deal with mental and

Many prisons have programs to help inmates complete their education, which aids in a successful transition back to society.

emotional issues, vocational instructors who prepare inmates for jobs after their release, chaplains who see to prisoners' spiritual needs, administrators and clerical staff, transportation personnel, legal pro-

A variety of mental health professionals and trained counselors help offenders successfully rejoin society after serving their sentences.

fessionals, and many other specialists. Instructors teach educational and vocational classes and oversee prison jobs, such as making furniture, license plates, and other products; servicing computers and other types of equipment; and operating print shops. Some educational professionals are assigned to help inmates acquire high school diploma equivalents and to learn advanced skills in clerical subjects, electronics, and languages.

Caseworkers and counseling specialists are needed at all government correctional levels to work with inmates, especially those whose sentences are coming to an end. Caseworkers manage an offender's case from sentencing to release. Counselors with different qualifications deal with inmates in specific areas, such as substance abuse, family problems, and employment.

As they reenter society, inmates face special challenges brought about by their time in confinement and their criminal records. Some people—including close relatives—will treat them as outcasts, even after they've served their time. It may be harder for them than for other applicants to obtain jobs. While they enjoy a great sense of freedom upon release, they also face stresses in adjusting to a lifestyle that's very different from what they've experienced behind bars. Many released offenders are unable to cope and, all too soon, return to the corrections system. This is called recidivism. Trained counselors can help them make successful transitions back to society.

Some prisons have programs to help inmates obtain professional credentials so they can be gainfully employed after their release.

Correctional treatment specialists are hired by government agencies, corrections facilities, and courts. They are counselors or caseworkers who meet with offenders, usually in their offices, to discuss and evaluate such matters as personal and family needs and problems, substance dependencies, job skills and employment training needs, and other concerns. Generally, these professionals hold at least a bachelor's degree in a social or behavioral science. The average annual salary for this type of position is about $50,000.

Counselors in juvenile corrections programs strive to provide guidance that will break the young offender out of what could become a lifelong criminal cycle. Often, the counselor and caseworker function as members of a team that might also include substance abuse professionals, vocational instructors, family service workers, health specialists, and probation staff.

The caseworker and counselor must have good management skills. Their tasks range from record keeping to budget planning, and report writing to policy making.

Advancement opportunities for counselors and caseworkers are varied. Supervisory roles are most common—directors, managers, and coordinators of corrections-related services, including halfway houses. Some counselors decide to focus their careers in specific areas where they think they can have the greatest positive influence: helping teenage offenders, working with substance-dependent offenders, or providing educational and vocational advice.

Medical workers, too, are vital members of correctional teams today. In times past, prisoners in many facilities received no medical treatment aside from the basic first aid that corrections officers or other inmates could provide. Outside doctors perhaps made periodic visits to examine inmates with severe conditions. Many prisoners languished and died of easily treatable medical problems.

THE PERFECT PETRI DISH

Even before the COVID-19 pandemic, prisons and jails provided the perfect environment for epidemics to take hold. Even though prisons are secure environments, people still go in and out every day. Staff commute to and from home. Inmates might need to be taken to court or to an outside medical facility. Vendors make deliveries and repair people come to fix things. Anyone coming into or leaving the prison environment can transmit illness without realizing it.

Many older prisons have outdated ventilation systems. Prisoners share bathroom and dining facilities. They don't have the luxury of bathing or laundering their clothing at will. Many have medical issues that can make them more susceptible to infectious disease. Maintaining proper security for dangerous inmates is a serious issue. The inmates have a right to medical care, and the medical team have a right to safety while doing their job.

Even the worst of convicted felons are entitled to medical care, but the incarcerated population is often the last segment of society considered in a health emergency.

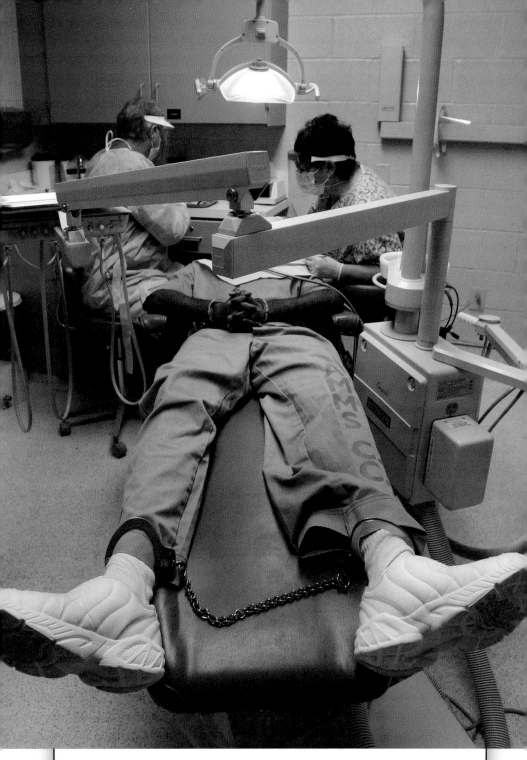

Even the most hardened offenders are entitled to proper medical care. Prisons must develop procedures to ensure that medical professionals are safe while doing their jobs.

TRAY PICK UP

Olympic gold medalist Misty Hyman speaks to female inmates at Perryville State Prison in Arizona about making a fresh start after being released from prison.

Today, regular medical staff members attend to inmates' health issues. Some doctors, nurses, dentists, and other medical professionals find that administering their talents and using their knowledge inside jails and prisons is especially rewarding. Of particular concern are aging prisoners who develop debilitating and terminal illnesses, and who must continue to serve time despite their conditions. In some prisons, hospices that provide special care and privileges are available for those who are in their final months or years of life.

HELPING OFFENDERS RETURN TO THE COMMUNITY

Halfway house staff must have many of the same skills as caseworkers and counselors. They work directly with offenders who've been released from prison but aren't entirely free yet. Halfway houses are temporary supervised residences within the community for prisoners who are nearing the end of their terms. The transitioning individuals must conform to the rules of the halfway house and satisfy the conditions of their release, such as completion of substance abuse programs, job assignments, and vocational training. Residents of the halfway house must demonstrate that they, indeed, are ready to return to society.

The halfway house manager must also know how to operate a correctional residence and run a business. The job involves staff management, budgeting, security and safety matters, upkeep of the facility, and an unending flow of paperwork.

Applicants for all of these jobs should keep in mind that although they're not primarily responsible for security, they're working with lawbreakers—people who've had to be removed from society. Even for counselors, who generally work inside their offices, away from the cell blocks, tense situations can arise that call for quick thinking.

THE PERSON RESPONSIBLE FOR EVERY DETAIL

For some corrections professionals, the ultimate goal of their career is to become warden of a facility. This is a long and complex process. Many wardens start out as corrections officers. They may work for decades before attaining the rank of warden. In addition to professional experience, wardens often hold undergraduate and graduate degrees in criminal justice or a related field.

Wardens are highly skilled professionals. They're responsible for the day-to-day administration of the entire facility—not just the penal programs. Everyone who does business with a prison, including delivery people, plumbers, and visitors, faces a much closer degree of scrutiny than they would in any other environment. The warden is responsible for understanding how every aspect of business or maintenance might impact the security of the facility.

Wardens must also be politically savvy. They need to understand the niche their facility occupies in their state's corrections system. It can be complicated to ensure total security of a facility, while also ensuring that inmates' human rights aren't violated, and maintaining a suitable public image. For example, it's illegal to segregate inmates by race, but many gang affiliations are racial, and mixing populations can result in violence for staff and inmates alike. It takes dedication, experience, and wisdom to navigate such difficult situations on a daily basis.

The average salary for a prison warden is about $88,000 per year. Of course, this may vary greatly depending upon the location of the facility. For many corrections professionals, the post of warden will be the last they hold before retirement. Some may go on to other government posts or choose to leave the corrections field entirely.

CHAPTER 4

HOW DO I GET STARTED?

While some positions in local prison systems might only require a high school diploma, someone pursuing a career in the corrections system should consider at least an undergraduate degree. This can be helpful if a civil service exam is required. Most federal corrections professionals hold degrees. A field of study pertaining to law or behavioral science is most helpful.

It's also good to bear in mind that newer prisons feature sophisticated technology. An officer processing prisoners may be taking biometric scans instead of simple fingerprints. The prison may be equipped with computerized cameras and electronic gates and doors. Prisons—and the people who staff them—have come a long way from the days of simple brick walls and iron bars.

WHICH MAJOR?

Appropriate college majors for prospective corrections officers include criminal justice, criminology, and police science. Other degrees that often lead to interesting corrections careers include sociology, social work, counseling, and psychology.

These high school students are studying the basic principles of the criminal justice system. Some may decide to pursue careers in law enforcement. Others may decide it's not the right field for them.

A college degree program will give the student a great breadth of understanding about corrections and criminal justice systems. Courses available to criminal justice majors vary from administration and economics to human behavior, pharmacology, safety, and telecommunications. The student will also study a selected foreign language and take basic courses including science, history, and English.

The objective of a college curriculum is to teach the aspiring criminal justice professional not only about the judicial and legal systems but also about a variety of subjects that will have a bearing in the workplace. Obviously, a graduate of such a degree program will enter the corrections workforce with a far greater knowledge of the job than those with limited educations.

Probation and parole officers in most systems must have bachelor's degrees in majors such as social work or criminal justice. Some agencies require postgraduate education. Experience is not required in some settings, but others call for one or more years of work in a related field, such as casework, the supervision of criminal offenders, or criminal investigation. Applicants should be able to communicate effectively with offenders from all backgrounds. Fluency in a second language is a plus.

A corrections counselor will need an education that focuses on psychology. These professionals need to understand the criminal mind and how to prevent recidivism. They also counsel individuals who have different types of personal problems—including

Officers and counselors involved in the parole process need to have a keen understanding of human nature. Their job is to help decide if an offender is ready to be returned to society.

substance dependence, uncontrollable anger, and various forms of psychological disorders. The counselor must know how to maintain an effective, safe counselor/client relationship with inmates. Some positions require past experience in conducting group counseling sessions.

For counseling specialists applying for federal corrections jobs, two years of graduate-level education in social or behavioral sciences is required, or a satisfactory combination of advanced study and experience.

Psychologists, doctors, nurses, and lawyers who commit to corrections-related careers must attain higher levels of education specific to their professions. Most psychologists in federal corrections systems hold doctoral degrees. They must diagnose and treat a variety of mental illnesses and emotional and personality disorders among prisoners. They also support the corrections staff, providing crisis and stress counseling, and helping to negotiate hostage situations and other conflicts. Besides their academic degrees, they must undergo corrections training at the Bureau of Prisons' academy in Glynco, Georgia.

Correctional facilities also employ clerical, maintenance, and other workers whose jobs require appropriate qualifications and training. Some corrections jobs call for weapons and self-defense expertise, but it's not necessary for other roles.

Although a bachelor's degree might not be required to obtain an exciting and rewarding job, young people interested in this career field should keep it in mind the future. A higher level of education improves the likelihood of advancement to better jobs, and it's often easier to obtain a college degree earlier in life than later. The worker who has earned a degree will likely receive quicker promotions and find a greater variety of job openings available. If a special area of corrections is of interest, additional

Although fluency in Spanish is always helpful, prospective students should inquire with the correctional system at which they wish to apply. There might be another language that's desirable in that particular part of the country.

education and training in that particular category will greatly improve job advancement potential.

There's an additional incentive for a prospective corrections worker to obtain an advanced degree or certificate: It tells the employer that the applicant is serious about a corrections career—serious enough to invest substantial time and money acquiring a suitable degree before even attempting to enter the job market.

OUTSIDE THE CLASSROOM

Besides their knowledge of the corrections process, law, and human behavior, corrections officers learn from on-the-job experience. They must understand the laws that apply in the prison and jail environment. They need to become thoroughly familiar with the policies of the institution where they work. They must be able to perceive personal traits and mannerisms of prisoners that might suggest trouble. For example, they must learn to recognize symptoms of substance use and subtle animosity that might exist between inmates. They also need to be sensitive to social issues, such as cultural and racial diversity. They must learn basic emergency response techniques—first aid, cardiopulmonary resuscitation (CPR), and firefighting, for example.

Corrections officers and workers in certain other areas of the corrections system will undergo training much like that of police officers. They must learn self-defense tactics and the use of different kinds of

These officers are undergoing physical training in a setting similar to a police academy. They will be taught to handle prisoners safely and within the boundaries of the law.

weapons. Naturally, they must stay in good physical condition. They must also possess certain essential personal traits, including the ability to respond appropriately and quickly in potentially dangerous situations, the ability to keep a cool head and calm outward attitude, and good organizational skills.

Officers who work with certain populations inside prisons require specialized training. With juvenile offenders, for example, the emphasis is on rehabilitation or correction, rather than punishment. The goal is to prevent the young person from committing any further crimes. Death row inmates present different challenges. There's often a long wait from sentence to execution, which takes a harsh mental toll. This is a very stressful environment for the staff as well.

Most bailiff positions require only a high school diploma or GED (General Education Development), unless the bailiff is a regular law enforcement officer, in which case the agency's normal educational requirements apply. Much of the bailiff's training— learning courtroom practices, terms, and special security needs inside a courthouse—is provided on the job by the court and/or the sponsoring law enforcement agency.

TRAINING AND EXPERIENCE

Like so many other fields, corrections is becoming more sophisticated. While it may be possible to secure an entry-level job in a local facility with a high school diploma, most institutions require candidates to undergo additional training.

Many prison systems have a training academy, similar to a police academy. Prospective corrections officers are expected to complete a course of academic and physical training before they're assigned to a facility. Once they're assigned, new hires are generally partnered with a more experienced officer. They might be considered on probation for as long as a year.

Corrections cadets undergo extensive physical training. They must be physically fit because of the very real possibility of having to pursue or subdue an inmate. They also receive training in self-defense and firearms, much like police cadets. Cadets must be familiar with the laws of the locality where they

ON THE JOB TRAINING AND MORE

Someone who's serious about a career in corrections might first consider enlisting in the armed forces. The Military Police and Internment/Resettlement Specialists receive similar training and experience to their civilian counterparts. This is in addition to physical conditioning and training in weapons and self-defense techniques. Military service also accustoms one to working with a team within a chain of command.

The military also has programs to help cover the cost of college tuition. The federal prison system makes an effort to hire veterans, and time served in the armed forces can count towards one's government service, helping to accumulate paid time off and other benefits more quickly.

A job as a security guard can provide valuable work experience necessary for a job in corrections.

work. Even convicted inmates retain some of their civil rights and officers must be aware of this and act accordingly.

Some systems require candidates to have previous job experience. Sometimes advanced degrees, life experience, or other job experience can substitute for prior experience in corrections. A job as a night security guard can provide familiarity with security protocols and technology. A position in inventory control demonstrates responsibility and an eye for details. Advanced computer or software knowledge is always useful. Fluency in more than one language, or a hobby such as target shooting can also count favorably. Emergency certifications such as first aid and CPR are a plus. Even work in IT or office administration demonstrates valuable skills.

Individuals interested in federal corrections jobs must possess at least a bachelor's degree, with graduate credits required for some levels of employment. Candidates are subject to rigorous screening and background checks. Successful applicants must complete a three-week training program at Glynco, Georgia, and receive 16 to 40 hours of additional training each year. Special consideration may be given to veterans of the U. S. armed forces.

A serious candidate with an eye toward a full and rewarding career in corrections should look upon education as an investment in the future. A college degree offers more opportunities for advancement in the corrections field and more options for a possible second career. Corrections is a mentally and physically demanding field. It can put a strain on family relationships. At some point, injury or stress might make a change attractive or even necessary. An officer with firsrthand experience working inside the prison system may become interested in influencing the system from the top. This might take the form of prison administration, law, or even politics.

Shown here is the official seal of the U.S. Federal Bureau of Prisons.

THE FEDERAL BUREAU OF PRISONS

The government agency in charge of our nation's prisons is the Federal Bureau of Prisons. Established in 1930, it was designed to create a prison system that was both more progressive and more humane to inmates. It provides a centralized administration for federal prisons. Furthermore, the bureau works to ensure prisons are safe, cost effective, and successful in helping inmates transition back into society.

The Federal Bureau of Prisons employs more than 37,000 professionals to supervise 154,000 inmates. It oversees numerous programs to aid in offenders' successful reintroduction to society.

CHAPTER 5

THE RIGHT CORRECTIONS CAREER FOR YOU

The best way to discover available corrections jobs is thorough Internet research. Government websites or corporate websites for private security firms will have the most up-to-date information available.

The Bureau of Labor Statistics lists two categories of corrections careers: "Correctional Officers and Bailiffs" and "Probation Officers and Correctional Treatment Specialists." As of 2020 they are predicting a 7 percent decrease in jobs for Correctional Officers and Bailiffs over the next 10 years. The bureau predicts a 4 percent increase in jobs for Probational Officers and Correctional Treatment specialists over the next 10 years. This tracks with news about states overhauling their criminal codes.

Most correctional institutions are government facilities with government staff. A good starting point is the official website of the state or municipality where you'd like to work. A state website will generally have a complete list of correctional facilities and programs. You can research the facilities that interest you and make informed decisions about which is the best fit for you—including factors such as how far you're willing to commute. The website will also include a listing of open positions, job requirements, civil service exams, and information on how to apply, as well as information on compensation and benefits.

Investigating a state's website will make you aware of all the options. If you're someone who prefers to work outdoors, you can see if there's a program similar to California's Conservation Camps in your area. If you like the idea of protecting society, but you're not sure about spending your entire career in a secured facility, you can see if your state utilizes independent contractors with special skills.

If you're interested in federal employment, you'll want to explore the Federal Bureau of Prisons website: www.bop.gov/jobs/. It lists open positions available throughout the country and includes detailed explanations of the application and hiring process. Each job listing provides a salary range and employment requirements, and details the possibility of promotion. The Federal Bureau of Prisons

The internet is where you'll do most of your career research. It's also almost certainly how you'll apply for jobs.

also utilizes volunteer mentors in its halfway houses and reentry programs.

You can also explore popular job search sites such as CareerBuilder and Monster. They list some government corrections jobs, as well as openings at private security companies. LinkedIn has listings for jobs in counseling and reentry assistance. Another source of job listings is newspaper classified ads, available online from many major publications.

WHAT HAPPENS WHEN YOU APPLY?

The applicant almost invariably will need to be a U.S. citizen who's at least 18 years old (21, for some jobs). Job applicants in most fields are subject to background checks. Prospective employers will want to verify the person's education and employment history and learn about possible firings, criminal charges, and workers' compensation claims. Employers commonly ask for character references.

The corrections applicant will face even closer scrutiny. Obviously, the applicant must have no felony record or problematic job history. A drug test almost certainly will be required, and a polygraph (lie detector) test might be administered. Background checks for certain corrections jobs are extensive and might include a review of driving records and credit reports as well.

Depending on their qualifications and skills, applicants will be called for an initial interview. Further interviews may be part of the hiring process.

You want to make a good first impression at any job interview, but for an interview in corrections, it's especially important to be punctual, professional, and neatly groomed.

The candidate also will be given a series of tests that might include a federal civil service test and a psychological test, depending on the nature of the job. Applicants for federal posts must also pass a Core Values Assessment. A physical is also likely to be required. The successful candidate might be hired almost immediately or might face a follow-up process that could take weeks or months.

Remember that when a job hopeful applies to a government agency or to a correctional institution, the application might be placed on file indefinitely. It could be weeks, months, or even years before the application rises to the attention of the hiring official for an appropriate job that becomes open. Applicants who seriously want to work for a particular corrections facility should periodically send their updated résumés to the hiring office.

New employees in corrections, as in most careers, work under probationary status for at least 90 days. Basically, that means they're in a trial period; they aren't considered permanent employees until they've proven they can handle the job. Trainees do not enjoy all the benefits of veteran employees. Their supervisors can dismiss them without having to document the reasons for dismissal, and the trainees might not be eligible yet to begin acquiring paid vacation time.

Federal facilities sometimes have immediate openings for certain locations. A recruitment bonus may be offered to applicants as incentive to work at those facilities.

LANDING THE JOB

Individuals with a serious interest in a corrections career should read extensively and investigate professional websites. Hollywood is poor reference material for this career choice. Contrary to what you might see in the movies, modern correctional facilities aren't looking to hire cowboys or "Rambos." They're seeking dedicated, conscientious professionals who work well in a team and have a serious interest in protecting society.

Job applicants should be clean cut and conservatively dressed. Arriving for an interview looking like an extra from an action movie is a sure-fire way to not be hired. Corrections officers need to project a demeanor of professional authority.

Applicants should be prepared to answer questions about their education and qualifications. They must be able to demonstrate a thorough understanding of the rigors of the job. They should also have researched the particular facility to which they're applying.

HOW MUCH CAN YOU EARN?

According to the Bureau of Labor Statistics, the average wage for correctional officers and jailers is about $50,000 per year. This will vary by location, with higher wages ($53,000–78,000) in states such as New York and California (where the cost of living is higher), and lower wages ($31,000–39,000) in southern and midwestern states. As most corrections jobs are civil service, they include a full benefits package, regular opportunities for advancement, and a retirement plan.

Wages at federal institutions run about $43,000–62,000 per year. Government facilities generally pay premium rates for Sundays and holidays worked, as well as night shifts. Due to the mental and physical demands of the job, there are nearly always openings for corrections officers. It's possible for a supervisor to earn as much as $100,000.

The median pay for probation officers and correctional treatment specialists is $58,000. These professionals are more likely to work in the community than in a corrections facility. This is an expanding job field, as some states are redefining what constitutes an incarcerable offense.

However the corrections field changes to adapt to the times, it'll always be necessary. The demanding nature of the profession is rewarded with competitive pay and benefits, and the knowledge that correctional workers protect society and help misguided individuals find their place in the community.

Once you've landed an interview with someone in the corrections system, it's important to be professional, courteous, and prepared. Make sure you have everything you need, including your résumé, references, and a concrete idea of what you want to ask the interviewer. Here are 10 great questions you can ask during your interview.

10 GREAT QUESTIONS TO ASK A CORRECTIONS EMPLOYER

1. Will I need any special training to become a prison guard?

2. Will I be expected to carry a firearm or other weapon?

3. What are my chances of being promoted and how long will that take?

4. What is the best position for me in the corrections system based on my experience?

5. Is there a chance I will experience violence or harm in this position?

6. What is the starting salary? Will I have a chance to increase it?

7. Do I need an undergraduate degree for this position or for a chance to be promoted?

8. Will I be expected to travel for this position?

9. Will I have a chance to transfer to another facility in the future?

10. Are there any positions available for people who like working outside?

CHAPTER 6

THE FUTURE OF CORRECTIONS

The corrections system is constantly being reimagined and redefined. In fact, many modern corrections systems and facilities don't have the word "prison" in their names—"corrections" and "rehabilitation" are more common. The idea of locking people away with no hope of reprieve is long outdated. Convicted criminals can't be sent overseas or imprisoned with no legal resources. All inmates are entitled to food, medical care, and sanitary living quarters. Even in the most extreme cases of violent inmates with no hope of parole, efforts are still made to provide education, spiritual comfort, and counseling.

Gone, too, are the days of dark and dirty cells. Contemporary detention facilities are built with

While no prison will ever be a pleasant place to be, modern facilities are designed to be secure and sanitary.

the latest technology. They are clean and sanitary. Electronic gates and doors, and computerized camera systems help to keep the staff safe and the facility secure. Modern communications systems allow the staff to keep in constant contact with all parts of the facility.

Computerized camera systems allow guards to monitor an entire facility while keeping distance between themselves and the inmates. Being able to spot trouble early helps keep everyone safe.

There's also a new recognition of the stress and physical risk associated with corrections work. Corrections officers are given comprehensive training for their jobs. Most benefits packages include medical insurance and employee assistance programs that provide support to the employee and their family. Counseling is available to officers in particularly stressful assignments, such as those who work with death row inmates.

UNDERSTAND WHAT YOU'RE GETTING INTO

A career in corrections is a solid job choice that will provide a good income. A desire to protect society and help wrongdoers to correct the course of their lives is a worthy goal. However, prospective job seekers need to approach the field carefully and with due diligence. They need to be very clear about the potential dangers of the job, as well as the stress and hours involved. Their pay and benefits will help support a family, but working nights, weekends, and holidays can put a strain on family relationships. The nature of keeping many people in close confinement means that contagious illness has always been a factor in correctional facilities.

However noble an officer's aspirations of helping offenders might be, they need to be aware that they'll encounter people who don't want help or perhaps are unable to accept it. They must be ever vigilant of the chance of violence in their workplace and the strain of working with people who resent their authority.

THE EVER-CHANGING NATURE OF CRIME AND CORRECTIONS

People who have set their sights on a career in corrections should follow news and current events diligently. American society is re-examining what constitutes a crime, and how crimes should be punished.

The so-called "War on Drugs" began in the early 1980s and caused the incarceration rates in the United States to skyrocket. Government officials chose to promote prohibition over reform or rehabilitation. This meant all forms of drug-related crimes—incuding the production, distribution, and use of drugs—were met with harsh sentences and fines. This, in turn, led to the construction of new prisons and the need for personnel to staff them. In addition to this, studies show that incarceration is not very successful in detering repeat drug offenders.

As evidenced by the results of various measures voted on in the 2020 elections, many Americans now consider drug use and possession to be social and medical issues rather than criminal ones. So how does that effect the corrections field? While there will unfortunately always be violent offenders who require secure confinement, current trends suggest that there will be an increasing demand for corrections professionals trained to assist in recovery and rehabilitation. The redefining of criminal codes is designed to keep people who have made a mistake or acted from desperation or on a reckless impulse out of the company of hardened violent criminals. The future of the corrections field may lie more in the realm of community supervision.

While some offenders will be people who made a mistake and wish to just get back to their lives,

Working in the corrections system is certainly not for everyone. The resposibilities are many, as are the dangers. However, it can also be very fulfilling to help protect and rehabilitate members of society.

others have behavioral issues that make violence second nature.

Correctional facilities and their employees are often under scrutiny from those outside the industry. Most institutions are government run, meaning they're funded by taxes. Taxpayers can be vocal—and often opposing—in their views. Many Americans feel that too many offenders are incarcerated for relatively minor crimes. Others will argue that convicted criminals are undeserving of any form of privileges, including anything beyond the most basic medical care. Groups such as the American Civil Liberties Union (ACLU) observe the conditions in prisons and bring legal actions for violations of inmates' basic rights.

As a corrections officer, you would be working in a high-stress environment with the constant threat of violence or injury. Your actions could be the subject of intense observation and debate. You would also be providing a valuable service to your community.

Myths and Facts About Working in the Corrections System

Myth: Prison guard is a good career choice for someone who wants to show off and boss other people around.

Fact: Prison guards need to be trusted team members. They're not only responsible for the security

The role of corrections officers is to protect society from violent offenders and help others try to find a place in the community once they've served their sentence.

of the facility, but also for respecting the inmates' basic human rights.

Myth: Women aren't allowed to be corrections officers.
Fact: While women have only achieved equality in the field in the late 20th century, they've long been involved in corrections. They've served as clerical workers, nurses, and matrons for female prisoners.

Myth: Convicted criminals have no rights.
Fact: Convicted felons may lose some of their civil rights, depending on where they live and the nature of their crime. These commonly include the right to vote, to serve on a jury, and possibly their parental rights.

Myth: Becoming a correctional officer is a deadend job.
Fact: There are many options available to people who start their career as a correctional officer. You may be promoted up the chain of command at a correctional facility. These positions may include sergeant, lieutenant, and captain. The higher you rise, the greter the responsibility. Guards may also work to become associate warden or warden. These positions require college coursework. Other guards may go on to become parole officers, correctional couselors, or youth counselors.

Myth: Convicted criminals do not deserve the same rights as other U.S. citizens.

Fact: Correctional employees know that prisoners deserve many of the same rights as reguar people. They deserve good medical and dental care. They deserve ways to improve themselves, such as schooling and counseling. They also deserve to be treated with respect from prison employees.

GLOSSARY

arsenal A collection of weapons.

contraband Forbidden items inside a prison, including phones, drugs, weapons, and objects from which weapons can be made.

detention centers Correctional facilities designed to house special categories of inmates, such as juveniles.

felony A serious crime punishable by imprisonment.

forfeiture The surrender of property as part of the punishment for a crime. Examples of confiscated items include weapons and vehicles that were used for transporting drugs or stolen goods.

GED General Educational Development (substitute for a high school diploma).

incarceration Confinement in a correctional facility.

itinerant Traveling from place to place.

jurisdiction The limits or territory within which a person or group can exercise authority.

marksmanship Exceptional skill with firearms.

misdemeanor A minor offense usually punishable by a fine, probation, or community service term.

moratorium A time when a particular activity is not allowed.

parole Early release from prison under supervised monitoring.

probation Suspension of a prison sentence or fine under the condition that the offender obeys supervisory rules.

recidivism A former prisoner's eventual return to criminal behavior after release.

rehabilitation The process of restoring an offender to a useful, law-abiding role in society.

restitution A court order for a thief or vandal to return stolen property or pay a victim the value of stolen or damaged property.

sentry An armed lookout, such as a sharp-shooter in a tower overlooking prison grounds.

warden Director of a prison.

warehouse To confine someone or some-thing with no short-term plans to move them elsewhere.

FOR MORE INFORMATION

American Correctional Association
206 North Washington Street, Suite 200
Alexandria, VA 22314
(703) 224-0000
Website: www.aca.org
Founded in 1870, the ACA is the oldest organization for corrections professionals.

American Probation and Parole Association
c/o The Council of State Governments
701 E. 22nd Street, Suite 110
Lombard, IL 60148
(859) 244-8207
Website: www.appa-net.org
The APPA is a leading professional organization for the community corrections industry.

Bureau of Justice Statistics
U.S. Department of Justice
810 Seventh Street NW
Washington, DC 20531
(202) 307-0765
Website: www.bjs.gov
This is the official source of information on prison populations. They publish numerous reports.

Correctional Service of Canada

340 Laurier Avenue W
Ottawa, ON K1A 0P9
Canada
(613) 992-5891
Website: www.csc-scc.gc.ca
This is the Canadian federal government agency that administers sentences of two years or longer. They're responsible for correctional facilities of various security levels, as well as community supervision.

CorrectionalOfficerEDU.org

Website: www.correctionalofficeredu.org/
A website of resources for people considering a career as a correctional officer. It includes descriptions of various jobs, information on salary, and educational requirements.

Federal Bureau of Prisons

320 First Street NW
Washington, DC 20534
Website: bop.gov
The Federal Bureau of Prisons is tasked with protecting society by confining convicted offenders in suitable facilities and guiding their reentry to society when appropriate.

FOR FURTHER READING

Bolles, Richard Nelson, et al. *What Color Is Your Parachute? For Teens, Third Edition: Discover Yourself, Define Your Future and Plan for Your Dream Job.* Berkeley, CA: Ten Speed Press, 2015.

Correction Officer Exam Study Guide. Test Prep Books, 2017.

Harr, J. Scott, and Karen M. Hess. *Careers in Criminal Justice and Related Fields: From Internship to Promotion.* 6th ed. Belmont, CA: Wadsworth Publishing, 2009.

Michigan State School of Journalism. *100 Questions and Answers About Police Officers, Sheriff's Deputies, Public Safety Officers and Tribal Police (Bias Busters Book 13).* Canton, MI: Front Edge Publishing, 2018.

Ross, Carroll J. and Michael Grace. *Guide to Getting a Federal Law Enforcement Job: Career Advancement, Internships and Entry Level Positions.* Independently Published, 2020.

Schroeder, Donald, and Frank Lombardo. *Barron's Correction Officer Exam*. 5th ed. Hauppauge, NY: Barron's Educational Series, Inc., 2020.

Titus, Alfred S. *The Personal Side of Policing: An In-Depth Look at How a Career in Law Enforcement Can Change and Affect Your Life*. Valley Stream, NY: A. Titus Consulting, LLC, 2018.

INDEX

A

administrator, 42, 50, 71, 72
Advanced Puppies for Parole, 37
American Civil Liberties Union (ACLU), 22, 90
architect, 43, 45
Arizona, 27
Attica Correctional Facility, 28

B

bail, 17
bailiff, 38, 39, 68
border patrol, 17
Bureau of Indian Affairs, 33
Bureau of Justice Statistics, 4, 39
Bureau of Labor Statistics, 44, 74, 80
Bureau of Prisons, 19, 21, 64, 73, 75, 77

C

California, 18, 23, 25, 26, 27, 75, 80
California Department of Corrections and Rehabilitation, 25
California Institute for Men at Chino, 26
California State Prison, Corcoran, 18
caseworker, 43, 51, 53, 57, 62
chaplain, 42, 43, 50
civil service exam, 60, 79
clerical work, 43, 64
college, 34, 44, 53, 58, 60, 61, 62, 63, 64, 66, 69, 71, 83
community service, 8, 19, 46
Conservation Camp, 23, 75
cook, 42, 43
Core Values Assessment, 79
Corona, Juan, 18
correctional treatment specialist, 53, 81
corrections officer, 24, 25, 27, 28, 30, 32, 33, 34, 36, 41, 43, 54, 58, 61, 74, 81, 90

ABOUT THE AUTHOR

Kathleen A. Klatte is the author of several nonfiction books for children and teens. Topics range from animals to constitutional law to even more animals. She also works as a costumer for historic sites and local theaters. Her credits include the short films *Runaway* and *The Misadventures of Ichabod Crane*, and the online documentary *People Not Property*, all for Historic Hudson Valley. Kathleen lives in New York with one cat and far too many books and Legos.

CREDITS